ANIMALS ON THE MOVE

UNDER THE GROUND

WRITTEN BY
Eliza Nodes

PowerKiDS press

Published in 2026
by The Rosen Publishing Group, Inc.
2544 Clinton Street, Buffalo, NY 14224

Written by: Eliza Nodes

Edited by: Rebecca Phillips-Bartlett

Designed by: Rob Delph

Cataloging-in-Publication Data

Names: Nodes, Eliza.

Title: Under the ground / Eliza Nodes.

Description: Buffalo, New York : PowerKids Press, 2026. | Series: Animals on the move | Includes glossary and index.

Identifiers: ISBN 9781499455861 (pbk.) | ISBN 9781499455878 (library bound) | ISBN 9781499455885 (ebook)

Subjects: LCSH: Animal migration--Juvenile literature. | Animal behavior--Juvenile literature. | Adaption--Juvenile literature.

Classification: LCC QL754.N634 2026 | DDC 591.568--dc23

Printed in China

CPSIA Compliance Information: Batch #QW26PK. For further information contact Rosen Publishing at 1-800-237-9932.

PHOTO CREDITS

All images are courtesy of Shutterstock.com, unless otherwise stated. Front Cover – onewildlifer, dugdax, Neil Bromhall, Karelian, Garna Zarina. 2&3 – IhorL, Wirestock Creators. 4&5 – alvarobueno, muratart, WilliamRoggero, Andriy Nekrasov. 6&7 – IhorL, jutamatk. 8&9 – Jurga Jot, Marigold Nix. 10&11 – Clint H, AwayWeGo50. 12&13 – Radiant Reptilia, ehrlif. 14&15 – Neil Bromhall, Danny Ye. 16&17 – Neil Bromhall, Danny Ye. 18&19 – Wirestock Creators, bayazed. 20&21 – Tsewang Gurmet, Robert Deller. 22&23 – Roman Samborskyi, Looka, Eric Isselee, Eric Isselee, Ganga Raj Sunuwar. Vectors throughout – rio2009.

CONTENTS

Words that look like this can be found in the glossary on page 24.

WHAT IS MIGRATION?

Migration is when animals travel from one place to another. Many animals above and below the ground migrate every year. Some animals migrate more than once a year. Some are always on the move.

Animals migrate for different reasons. They might migrate:

- To avoid challenging weather
- Because of changes to their habitat
- To find food and water
- To find somewhere to have their young

Let's have a look at some underground animals that migrate.

THE EARTHWORM WRIGGLES UP AND UP

Earthworms live in many parts of the world, but they do not migrate very far. In autumn, earthworms wriggle deep down into the soil. This helps them to avoid freezing or drying out when the earth gets icy.

In spring, earthworms travel upwards until they reach the surface. Earthworms can move faster above the ground. Earthworms migrate to find a mate, find a new place to live, and to avoid predators.

So they do not dry out, earthworms migrate above ground when it is wet.

Earthworm migration is being affected by humans. Some worms end up in soil that is then used in plant pots and compost bags. These are often sent to other countries.

Different types of earthworms have been found in countries they should not be in. Earthworms are good for their natural habitats. However, they can harm environments they do not belong in.

This earthworm is in the wrong habitat and above the ground in winter.

THE RATTLESNAKE'S SLITHERY MISSION

Rattlesnakes migrate twice a year. In the summer, they travel to their feeding and breeding grounds. Then, they migrate back to their dens in time for winter.

Pregnant rattlesnakes live together. They care for their young and babysit for others.

Rattlesnakes travel along migration corridors. Migration corridors are routes that the snakes follow to and from their dens. Houses and roads have been built on these routes. This has caused problems between rattlesnakes and humans.

Snakes are cold-blooded. That means they need to stay warm to live. In summer, the roads that cross migration corridors get hot. Snakes rest on the roads to warm up. This means the snakes can get run over by cars.

Rattlesnake fences stop rattlesnakes from reaching their breeding grounds.

People have put safety measures in place on rattlesnake migration corridors. One safety measure is road signs. Some roads are closed twice a year so snakes can cross them safely.

THE NAKED MOLE RAT'S EXPEDITION

Naked mole rats are pink, nearly hairless rodents. They are almost blind and spend most of their lives in underground tunnels. They are mostly found in East Africa.

Naked mole rats get their water by eating the underground parts of plants.

Naked mole rats live in groups called colonies. The leader of the colony is called the queen. She is the only female that produces young. The other females help take care of the queen's young.

A naked mole rat queen can have up to 27 young at a time.

Sometimes, naked mole rats leave their colony. They do this so they can have their own young. When they leave, they migrate above ground to create a new colony.

New colonies are usually started far away from others. This keeps them safe from attacks. A new colony can be made without mole rats migrating. This happens when the queen dies and another female becomes queen.

THE HIMALAYAN PIKA'S HIKE

Himalayan pikas are small mammals. They live high up in the Himalayan mountains, so they do not cross paths with people very often. Pikas are cute, but they have to be tough to survive in the mountains.

In summer, pikas collect grass and wildflowers. They lay them just outside their rocky dens to dry in the sun. They save these plants to eat in the winter.

Himalayan pikas can get too hot and overheat quickly. To stop this from happening, they migrate to higher, cooler ground in the summer. However, climate change is causing problems for their migration and habitat.

It is getting so warm that some pikas' winter dens are on mountain tops. This means there is nowhere cooler to go in the summer. The plants pikas eat cannot grow if it is too hot.

WHAT HAVE YOU LEARNED?

Now that you have learned about underground animals that migrate, let's put your knowledge to the test. Grab a pencil and some paper. It is quiz time!

QUESTIONS

1. What time of year do earthworms migrate up?

2. How are people trying to protect rattlesnakes?

3. What color are naked mole rats?

4. What do Himalayan pikas eat?

Answers:

1. Spring
2. By putting up road signs and closing roads
3. Pink
4. Grass and wildflowers

GLOSSARY

BREEDING GROUNDS	the places where animals make and produce their young
CLIMATE CHANGE	a change in the typical weather or temperature of a large area
COMPOST	rotten material that is added to soil to help plants grow
ENVIRONMENTS	parts of the natural world
HABITAT	the natural home in which animals, plants, and other living things live
MAMMALS	animals that are warm-blooded, have a backbone, and produce milk to feed their children
MATE	a partner of the same species that an animal produces young with
PREDATORS	animals that hunt other animals for food
RODENTS	animals, such as rats, mice, and squirrels, that have long front teeth which grow throughout their whole lives

INDEX